This book is 'light on a dark night of one soul'. It is a brave narrative of a difficult period in the life of an author. Elaine Brown will blush to read this, but those who read her story will find it to be true.

Tom Houston

This is a brave book full of practical help as well as some very deep spiritual insights. It came to me at a time of great personal suffering, and all I can say is that it helped me a great deal, so I guess it will most certainly help others in the same boat. There are not many people brave enough to write in such detail about such a difficult period in their lives, but Elaine's honesty and openness will, I know, bless many as I myself have also been blessed though reading her book.

Jennifer Rees-Larcombe

So Strange A Road

Learning to Live
with Depression

Elaine Brown

Christian Focus

© Elaine Brown
ISBN 1 85792 180 1
Published in 1997
by
Christian Focus Publications,
Geanies House, Fearn, Ross-shire,
IV20 1TW, Great Britain

CONTENTS

INTRODUCTION

These past months have been baffling in the extreme. A depressive illness is often much harder to bear than a physical complaint, its distress the greater because few people understand. As a result the sufferer feels very alone, and wonders if there is anyone else at all who, from personal experience, can identify with their pain.

What a relief it has been to discover that there are such people! I have needed to know that and perhaps you do too. So I've written this booklet simply to say 'You are not alone. I feel for you because I know what it is like.' I should add that this is very much a personal story and some aspects of my journey will be different from yours. I am sure, however, that there will still be common ground, enabling us to identify with one another.

Maybe this story will offer you some comfort and reassurance and that will make the challenge of writing it worthwhile. I also wanted to share those factors which have helped and those which haven't, as I've travelled this difficult stretch of the route. Such guidelines might be of use to anyone seeking to help a person suffering from a depressive illness.

How much I have valued the love and understanding of my husband and three grown children, also the skill and sympathy of my doctor, and the kindness shown by many friends. All have been strong evidence to me of God's concern and constant care.

1. SO STRANGE A ROAD

A few years ago we were travelling along a major motorway. At one point it divided in two, southbound traffic to the left, northbound to the right. As we branched on to our required route I glanced down at the markings on the road and realized that the crucial dividing point began with a single block of white paint. Just one mark, followed by a succession of others, leading traffic away on to two entirely different routes. Soon several hundred yards would separate the motorways and eventually they would be miles and miles apart. Yet it had all begun with that single small block of paint.

'A parable?' I wondered as we continued on our route. To me it seemed to indicate that the starting point of a major turn in life may well appear just as insignificant.

I know now that this has been true for me, though only recognized in retrospect. I attached little significance to those first niggling physical symptoms. Weakness and nausea. Then tiredness and some pain. It was autumn and as the long dark evenings drew in I decided that the damp, chilly weather could well make a person feel under par. Christmas came and went. The symptoms increased. In February I saw the doctor and not long afterwards was admitted to hospital for weight loss and a pancreas problem. It had all happened quite quickly and, since I had already had a brush with liver cancer, I was very afraid.

So many thoughtful people assured us of their prayers, and the night before admission, our minister and two close friends joined me and my husband, Les, for a valued time of prayer and anointing with oil, as suggested in James' New Testament letter (5:14). One of these friends quietly told me, 'I've had a picture of you as a very small, needy person, yet safely enclosed in the arms of a very big Father.' How much that picture meant! I reached out to its comfort over and over again during the following weeks.

Hospital wasn't nearly as bad as I had feared, and visits from Les and several friends cheered me on anxious days. Best of all the tests showed no sinister cause for my symptoms. What a relief! And what strong, happy expectations began to fill my mind. I would soon be well again! God's healing may not have come instantaneously, as requested, but that would not make it any less valuable in the end. Early one morning, as dawn broke, I caught sight of the morning star shining in through a high pane of the ward window. Such a strong symbol of hope! It made my day, and was also remembered for many another day afterwards.

A regime of medication was begun and I was allowed home after ten days. What a home-coming! I had hardly been back a day or two before the sitting room was filled with flowers, plants and cards. Friends called, food was kindly brought, and I soon felt overwhelmed – much humbled too – by the love and thoughtfulness so generously expressed. I was receiving careful medical care, both from the consultant and our GP, and although still weak, was confident of full recovery. Such a good feeling!

*****

One of my two close friends (they were to become prayer partners with me) lent an Episcopal prayer book and there, in the Litany, I found these words from Psalm 91:4: 'He shall cover thee with his feathers, and under his wings shalt thou trust.'

What a tender portrayal of God's care! It became another of my favourite 'mind pictures' – a small, vulnerable nestling sheltered safely under the protective feathers of the parent bird. I needed this picture when beset by the frustrations of slow recovery. Oh to be quickly fit and active, efficient and productive once again! But God was working to a different time scale. For the present he wanted me to nestle, not wrestle. That was hard! I didn't realize how important such a nestling would soon prove to be.

Spring crept in, colourful with snowdrops, crocuses and daffodils. Bluebells too. The nearby woods were full of them! Here in the north April and May give particular joy but this year something strange was happening. I couldn't get into the happy mood, even though I was becoming stronger. Nor was I coping with simple things like preparing food, or shopping. Favourite recipes failed (at meal times we struggled through flat sponges, tough pastry, the lot!) and I became over-anxious when faced with row after row of goods in the supermarket. Which size of loaf should I choose? How many jellies should I buy? Easy decisions were now so difficult. My mind wasn't functioning in its usual confident way. It was a new and extremely unwelcome development. Things like this just didn't happen to me.

To ease the situation I simplified menus and cut out most baking. Les spared time from his home-based printing work to help at the supermarket. It was important for me still to go shopping, still to work around the house, still to do 'my' things. Les sensed this and remained tactfully available when I needed him. Any take-over, however kindly meant, would have undermined confidence still further.

About this time a letter arrived from a fellow we hadn't seen for years. 'May I come for about ten days at the end of the month? Things have been rough. I'm in a mess and need a break.' For some reason that threw me. (Why? Offering hospitality had always been such a pleasure.) Now I was afraid I wouldn't cope, not only when it came to meals, but also with giving the special care our friend would require. I worried for days, then felt guilty. His need was far greater than mine, so couldn't I be glad to help and take care of him? He came, fitted in immediately, appreciated all I served up, and quietly shared some of his difficulties as we sat talking in the evenings.

May had come and it was more than time to prepare the garden for bedding plants. 'I'll do it!' he volunteered. 'Gardening is my big love!' So that's how he spent much of his holiday and, before leaving, all the flower beds were planted out. 'It's done

11

me a world of good being here!' our friend commented as he left. He didn't know that he'd done me a world of good too, just by being so easy-going and thoughtful.

The need to be there for him had taken me right out of myself. That was valuable. God had lovingly helped me as a result of his visit. 'Maybe everything's going to be fine from now on' I thought happily as I rested in the garden one afternoon, admiring the first bright blooms on the petunias.

Why am I so sad?
Why am I so troubled?
I will put my hope in God,
and once again I will praise him,
my saviour and my God

(Psalm 43:5, Good News Bible).

*****

'Once again' I did praise him – that afternoon – but there were to be quite different 'once agains' when I was too distressed to do so and could only nestle beneath his protective wings. How completely God understood. I needed to remember that, particularly when feeling bad about lack of my usual happy spirit. I began to find work around the house irksome, and had to force myself to keep to usual standards. (Why such disinclination? I generally found pleasure in being a housewife.) Nor was I able to attempt a return to a writing programme. My mind wasn't sharp enough and I hadn't written an article for months. I put this down to on-going physical weakness, aware that, in the past, physical illness had always dulled my thinking processes.

Each gradual development added up to something very strange. Before all this I'd considered myself a placid, easy-going person. Outgoing and optimistic too. Things didn't get me down, but they did now. Early mornings were sometimes hard. Always before I had leapt out of bed, eager to start the day but now I woke with dark apprehension. How was I going to cope? It was helpful to turn to well-loved Bible verses as the day began and they came to mean more to me now than ever before:

'...fear not, for I am with you,
    be not dismayed, for I am your God;
I will strengthen you, I will help you,
        I will uphold you with my victorious right hand'
                                    (Isaiah 41:10, RSV)

I sat in bed and let my mind linger with those words. Often, as I did so, I found myself glancing at a plaster figure on the bookshelf. It was given by a friend and depicts a shepherd carrying a lamb, while its mother follows trustfully alongside. That simple figure, together with the Bible verses, steadied my mind. I was able to start the day aware that I was not alone. Jesus was with me. He knew what lay ahead. He would help me as I stayed close. I tried to talk briefly with him through the day – as I washed-up at the sink, prepared food, sat down to write a letter, visited a friend. If I made some silly, uncharacteristic mistake, or anxiously dithered over a trivial decision, it meant much to know that Jesus was there to steady and reassure me with his right hand. It eased the fear of what was happening – and the frustration.

Not that all mornings were hard, just some of them. There were many relaxed starts to the day when I felt good and wondered why on earth I'd let things get me down on previous occasions. 'How ridiculous that I should have felt like that!' I'd chide myself as I got dressed, determined that from now on there would be no such further blips; everything would return to normality. Yes, there were lots of good days too, when everything went fine. For this reason I didn't mention my harder patches to anyone, not even to the doctor or close friends. Only Les knew.

2. NO U-TURNS!

The Christian life ... is a continual discovery
of Christ in new and unexpected places
(Thomas Merton).

Summer came, bringing with it drifts of wild flowers along the river bank beyond the back garden. The
scent of meadowsweet and wild roses filled the air,
and soft winds rustled through the tall beeches on
the far side of the water. Glorious weather! Hot too.
In fact the garden began to wither, despite Les' ef-
forts with the hose. I felt sad every time I looked at
the flower beds, so carefully planted out. Even the
petunias were shrivelling. This year, for some reason, the sight greatly distressed me. I couldn't bear
to see the garden so parched. Everyone else's flowers seemed to have fared far better and I envied my
friends their colourful borders. How odd to be so
envious. Always before I'd enjoyed their gardens as
much as our own. Now it was hard to find pleasure
in them, or even in the beautiful public gardens in
the city. I noticed, also, that my spontaneous appreciation of loveliness had diminished. I had to make
myself notice the beauty of wild flowers, woods, the
far hills. Yet, there were brief snatches of intense
pleasure, as if God wanted to make up for my difficulties by concentrating all those missed moments
of appreciation into one sweet encounter of delight.
One summer evening I passed the honeysuckle in

our garden, strong with fragrance, and as I paused to examine a single trumpet flower, its delicate scent immediately cheered me. A touch of God's refreshing aromatherapy as the day ended? Certainly it was a discovery of Christ in an unexpected place.

*****

The long, sunlit evenings often tempted us out for a drive and a stroll and we valued those times together in the peaceful countryside. Then, on one such sunny evening, as we left the village, I felt a shadow coming over me, a mental darkness that stole all happiness, replacing it with cold foreboding. Foreboding of what? I didn't know. It was such a sudden, distinct feeling that I can only liken it to being given an intravenous injection of a most unwelcome substance. It brought about an immediate inner difference, and was the first of many such episodes during the following months. I have often wondered if it is due to the release of a chemical into the bloodstream since its effect is so rapid, marked and inescapable. There is nothing I can do to counteract its alien influence, only wait until, hours later, the darkness slowly lifts.

Fortunately such experiences were occasional at first. There were many good times over those summer weeks, many enjoyable evening drives in the countryside. Times of fun with friends, as well, when the darkness was completely forgotten, and other symptoms dismissed as trivia. After all, I was still

16

physically weak, tired, and nauseated at times and that could explain difficulties on the mental front. The thought of a depressive illness never entered my head. Weren't people mostly tearful and mopey when depressed? I didn't suffer from those symptoms – and was mostly spared them later on – so there was no point in mentioning these other mental blips to the doctor during physical check-ups. I did tell Les about the sudden dark episodes, though. It was helpful to put feelings into words and thus find a measure of relief. I hoped he didn't mind.

My two prayer partners continued to call in regularly to pray for physical recovery when this seemed slow in coming. I valued their kindness and prayer-care very much. Through them God gave new strength and hope. Quite a few other friends also assured me of their prayers and shared quotations, and I was touched that they should continue to remember me in this way as the weeks went by. Here are some of the words friends gave me:

Every day, every hour, every moment
has been blessed by the strength of his love.
At the turn of each tide
he is there at my side,
and his touch is as gentle as silence

(E. White).

We will lift up our eyes to the hills –
where does our healing come from?
Our healing comes from the Lord,
the maker of heaven and earth.

The Lord will bring us his salvation –
he will heal our lives completely;
the Lord will watch over our coming and going
both now and for evermore.

(Adapted from Psalm 121)

*****

Summer was on the wane. Looking out at the
parched, colourless garden I felt glad that we would
soon be able to dig the flower beds over and forget
the sorry sight they'd presented over recent weeks.
Harvest had come early and most of the fields were
already reaped. The last, lingering oyster-catchers
foraged in the stubble before flying back to the coast,
and other birds started to flock. The robin presented
us with his tuneful autumn song as he sat at the top
of next door's roof and, for some reason, the owls in
the woods became very vocal each evening – sometimes during the day as well. On one of our evening
drives upriver we noticed that the large osprey nest
wedged into the top branches of a gaunt old tree
seemed deserted. The parent birds and their two
fledged young had left already for the warmth of
north Africa. Yes, summer was slowly dying and the
first vivid golds of autumn shone out in the lingering sunlight.

For me, life now became very unpredictable. The
dark patches sometimes lengthened to fill the whole
day, but there would be a few good days in between.
It was frustrating to be so much at the mercy of this
distressed state of mind. A friend wrote perceptively:

'Feeling better one day, feeling bad the next. It's like a sunny or a rainy day, but without a forecast.' Yes, there was no advance notice, but at least the sunny days still predominated. A new feature of the dark times were the irrational fears which swamped my mind; a further development from the earlier loss of confidence. The smallest problem, or possible problem, suddenly assumed huge, almost insurmountable proportions filling me with anxiety. I just couldn't get the matter out of my mind. This led to guilt in the light of reassuring words from the Bible: 'Fear not, for I am with you'; 'Be still, and know that I am God'; 'Cast all your anxieties on him, for he cares about you.' How often in the past I had shared those words with anxious friends, confident that they would be helped. Now I tried hard to cling to them myself, but the ridiculous, irrational fears persisted, powerful and pervasive. The GP was now well aware of my difficulties and during one visit I talked about these fears. 'But that's how it is with a depressive illness,' the doctor explained. 'Everything is out of proportion. Your mind just isn't working normally and there's no point in trying to reason with it.' I found that helpful and it eased the guilt. In fact, guilt was completely uncalled for anyway. God wasn't standing over me waving an accusing finger. He understood my mental condition, made constant allowances for it, and merely wanted me to take refuge in his compassion. Some psalm words helped me considerably and I still often think of them and the tender picture they portray:

Lord, I have given up my pride...
I am not concerned with great matters
or with subjects too difficult for me.
Instead, I am content and at peace.
As a child lies quietly in its mother's arms,
so my heart is quiet within me.

(Psalm 131:1, 2, GNB)

The doctor had deliberately used the description 'depressive illness' but the word 'depressive' didn't penetrate. It was too hard to take on board. 'Not coping' was a much easier way of saying it. I did, however, note the 'illness' bit, maybe because it fitted with that physical feeling of being 'injected' with some strange substance.

*****

To counteract the fears and apprehensions I tried to concentrate on the exciting holiday we had been planning over many months. In late September we were to fly to Vancouver, Canada, to visit Les' relatives. After this our itinerary would take us to the eastern seaboard of USA to see one of our sons, and finally to Florida where my sister had offered us her holiday flat. The entire trip was due to last for three weeks and now, at last, it was looming ahead. But, frustratingly, I couldn't get into the holiday mood. Sometimes I wondered about being able to cope physically with such a trip, but mostly I was afraid of the mental and emotional demands it would make.

On the other hand, maybe a good long holiday would bring about the cure for which I longed? The doctor, whilst recommending a break, wasn't hopeful about this.

To take my mind off holiday apprehension I worked hard around the house to complete the autumn cleaning. It's something I do every year, usually with no trouble, but this time round it required strict discipline to make myself work through one simple task a day. What a happy relief when I ticked the last item off the cleaning list! I enjoyed the sense of satisfaction and was glad I hadn't given up. House cleaning was at least something I could do when much, outside the home, was beyond my capabilities. Not that church and village activities were a factor at the time anyway. Most groups had closed down over the summer, and autumn programmes had yet to begin. I was glad of this, aware of being now incapable of playing my usual cheery part. Furthermore, since groups weren't meeting no one would know of the problem. I often took comfort from the fact that few people were 'in the know'. It was not that I felt ashamed of the illness (I didn't, and never have) but that I feared a lack of understanding. It was a happy surprise to discover, much later on, that quite a few could relate closely to my depressed state. I had had no idea that they'd once travelled a similar route, simply because, like me, they had so carefully camouflaged their condition at the time.

Several weeks earlier I had looked out a slip of paper kept in one of our files. It was entitled 'A First

Aid Kit when you are feeling low'. Although a 'low' is not nearly so overwhelming as a depressive illness, I wanted to consider at least some of the suggestions made. Here they are:

1. Gather together a small collection of Bible verses which give comfort and reassurance. Read these slowly and carefully when you are feeling down. Let the words calm and strengthen you.

2. Make a cup of tea and sit down for a while, listening to a favourite piece of music. Care for yourself!

3. Relax and start reading a long anticipated book.

4. Phone a friend and ask if you can call in for a little while. If possible, walk to her house through the fresh air.

The Kit then listed some of Martin Luther's personally tried advice when he was going through a 'low':

Avoid being alone for long periods.

Seek out people or situations which bring you pleasure.

Sing and make music.

Deliberately dismiss heavy thoughts.

Make a list of all the things for which you *can* give praise, despite all.

Exercise patience with yourself.

Believe that depression *can* have a positive, fruitful side.

To these I added three others:

visit someone each day, or invite them round for coffee;

do something for someone each day;

get out and about in the fresh air each day.

The First Aid Kit and Martin Luther's suggestions were helpful, though difficult to achieve at times, specially when it came to deliberately dismissing heavy thoughts, and giving praise. I tried to concentrate on giving thanks to God at the end of the day, letting my mind go back over the hours to identify particular scenes or events which had lifted me a little. But it was hard, not least because I was very tired in the evenings. It was better to thank him there and then during the day, as soon as I recognized one of his special touches. Sometimes Les and I would sing rather than pray before a meal, using the verse of a praise hymn, such as:

All good gifts around us are sent from heaven above, then thank the Lord, O thank the Lord, for all his love.

As Luther had mentioned, singing was helpful – I tried to sing when working around the house, but it didn't come naturally. Visiting someone each day, or doing something to help another person (simple baking, making soup, writing a letter or card, making a phone call, fetching shopping) also proved exacting at times because of tiredness and disinclination. But

I wanted, as far as possible, to keep to this practical plan because it prevented me from becoming self-absorbed. (Self-centredness has been a fear all along. I need constantly to counteract it.) Also, I found that, despite any initial reluctance to visit or to care for someone, I usually gained from following through on the plan. After many a visit I came home refreshed and encouraged simply by being with other people, and talking about their lives and situations. It put things in perspective and gave a touch of normality to the day. For all this I had begun to realize that, much as I wished it were possible, there could be no reversal of what was happening in my life. No U-turn. I had become the victim of a condition more distressing than I had ever known before. And it was getting worse. That was frightening. I tried not to think about it. 'Just live one day at a time' I'd tell myself, but that was much easier decided than done, and hardly ever achieved. The dark, heavy fears made sure of that.

3. FURTHER ALONG THE ROUTE

Sorrow is God's greatest opportunity to deal with us.
Because in those times we are so defenceless.
We know that we simply can't continue on our own
(Ethel Renwick).

September had begun but it was still warm enough
to eat breakfast outside, or to lie out on the lawn in
the early afternoon. On better days I valued time to
relax back and look up into the cloudless blue sky.
Sometimes a couple of gulls would circle high above,
and I loved to watch as their plumage became
glistening white with each turn. Gazing upwards, I
would consider the limitlessness of God. He was way
above and beyond that all-encompassing sky. So
immensely great! – and yet involved with my small
life, knowing me far better than I knew myself. It
was reassuring to think of that. Nowadays it had
become hard to concentrate for long on Bible reading,
particularly more complex passages so, during early
morning reading times, I set such sections aside and
read through one of the simpler gospels instead. Jesus
was real in those pages and real to me now, too, as I
lay out in the sunshine. I needed those times of
reassurance in preparation for other times when I felt
utterly defenceless, at the mercy of alien influences
in my life.

At a regular physical check-up the doctor referred
to the depression, now so obvious. It was linked to

the earlier pancreas problem, apparently, and was likely to take a while to clear. 'We may need to try anti-depressants,' the doctor continued but, after discussion, we decided to wait a while in the hope of spontaneous recovery. 'Did I feel guilty, as a Christian, about having a depressive illness?' the doctor then asked. I could honestly answer 'No' but I did feel guilty about being unable to take my usual part in activities within the church and community. These had now started and autumn programmes were in full swing. I felt bad that I could not help out, thus adding to the workload of others. This had been an on-going struggle, but at least I had been able to continue with one or two commitments, and the doctor pointed this out to encourage me. 'Don't do too much though. Don't take on anymore,' I was warned. I could see the sense of this but sometimes it was hard precisely to identify what I could manage and what I couldn't. I longed for the encouragement of finding that I *could* rise to some small extra demand, and yet if I failed at it disappointment ran deep, setting me back several steps. I still need to feel my way carefully in this area and, after quite a few failures, am now more cautious.

After the doctor's appointment I pondered the fact that, as with a surprisingly large number of other sufferers, I don't have any of the usual reasons to be depressed; I haven't been bereaved, I'm not up against a stressful situation at home or at work, no big demanding changes have occurred. It's simply that I've been physically ill, and this is largely responsible for so bewildering an aftermath. I long to be completely well again, in body and mind. Will that day come soon? If only it would!

*****

Around this time I decided to try the 'mind over matter' approach on waking one morning and determined to live the day ahead as if I was quite normal. Even to have considered this possible showed how little I'd grasped the extent of my problem, but I saw it as a way of fighting back against the now more frequent despair. Later that day I set off across country to a coffee meeting at a friend's house and found myself automatically appreciating the loveliness of the fields and hills bathed in gentle September sunshine. Such spontaneous pleasure was a good sign. By the time I reached the house I felt encouraged, more able to face a roomful of people, but an hour or so later I felt I must leave and slipped quietly out during the prayer time. It had taken considerable effort to give a normal impression to those present and I needed time to recover. On any other day I would have gone home to do so, as wisely advised. ('Don't take on too much.') But this was a 'mind over matter day' when I was determined to do normal things, and visiting a friend for lunch was part of the plan. Being with her was enjoyable, for a little while, but then I began to get inwardly agitated at being away from home so long. Concentration on conversation required increasing effort, and in the end I excused myself and set off. I was completely spent and, once back, could only lie on the bed and weep at my failure. The effort of trying to be normal had proved far too much. Les left his printing and came and sat with me for a while, offering a gentle rebuke followed by reassurance. Then he prayed for me. How much that meant! I had foolishly attempted a plan way beyond my capabilities. It was hard to accept the fact that, when struggling with an abnormal condition, you cannot make yourself normal however hard you try. A humbling realization too. As I lay back for a little longer God's words to Joshua came to mind:

It is the Lord who goes before you;
he will be with you, he will not fail you or forsake you;
do not fear or be dismayed

(Deuteronomy 31:8, RSV).

I knew then that it was important to keep following behind the Lord rather than rushing ahead with my own determined plans. Only then could I be protected by his closeness and faithful care. I learned a thing or two that day, the hard way, and there were to be further occasions when I would have to learn the same lesson all over again. Illness is so hard to accept.

About that time a simple touch from God became very valuable to me. Sometimes it was still hot enough to sleep on top of the bed with only the light bedspread for a covering. One morning I woke feeling very low. I just didn't want to start the day, so instead snuggled down and wrapped the spread tightly round me. As I did so there was a sense of God speaking to me. 'Don't be afraid to get up,' he

28

seemed to say. 'Let me wrap you round with my presence and you will be safe in my care.' What a difference that strong assurance made! – and the remembrance of its truth has often helped on difficult mornings since.

*****

Reluctance to start the day was largely due to the fact that, because of the illness, I didn't have specific writing work to do now. The hours ahead lacked purpose and I missed the challenge of tackling a given project until successful completion was achieved. I longed for a work programme and, to my dismay, found myself envying those who had a daily job to go to ... our daughter with her radiography, a friend with her counselling ministry, mothers with children to care for, friends working in frontline situations overseas. I felt useless, set aside, not required any more. That wasn't true, however, and I needed to remind myself of the fact.

Over the years God had drawn me into a ministry of intercession and I'd come greatly to value the opportunity for quiet prayer after lunch each day. This *was* something I could still do. Not that long, concentrated prayer was possible now, due to poor concentration, but I continued to find pleasure from working through a prayer request file and briefly remembering people and situations before God. 'Mention prayers' you might call them. Sometimes, when friends visited, I asked them to let me know of anything I could note down to remember in prayer, and it was also possible to gather prayer request booklets from various caring groups. Intercession has become a source of ongoing pleasure, a time to be close to God, and it has helped to put some purpose into each day. Also, it gives the opportunity prayerfully to 'visit' several different people and situations, and this has the valuable spin-off effect of taking me out beyond the confines of my own home and circumstances. It is also possible to read a small section of a devotional book during these quiet times. (Nothing heavy, I can't cope with complexities yet.) What good companions such books have been!

It was interesting that, in those early autumn days, I often fell asleep during times of prayer and reading, even though I was blessed with deep sleep each night. 'Sleep is something to be grateful for at any time of the day,' the doctor reassured. 'Most depressed people struggle with insomnia.' So Les and I started to joke about the afternoon cat-napping, though it was hard often to awake to the same dark despair that now frequently afflicted me in the mornings. 'Call me when you feel like that,' Les offered, 'and I'll pray with you.' That proved important when I awoke mid-afternoon, for I was troubled about having nothing to do for the rest of the day. Purposelessness was definitely a part of the blackness and it was helpful, once we'd prayed, to chat about how I could fill the following hours. A visit? Some simple cooking? Maybe a shopping trip to the nearest town? And then, too, there were the needed preparations for our holiday....

4. ACROSS THE ATLANTIC

It was late September, and still hot! Our holiday departure had come at last! Somehow I'd managed to work through all the 'to be done' lists and now the suitcases were lined up by the front door. Ever since my childhood travel has been a cause for great excitement. This time I felt strangely subdued, but determined, none the less, to enjoy the 3-week trip. After more than eight hours in the air we reached Vancouver, to be warmly welcomed by Les' relatives, with whom we spent ten days. It was good to relax at their home, to take a few trips around the city and, on one occasion, to drive along remote upriver stretches of the Fraser River. We even travelled across to scenic Vancouver Island to visit close friends but, although we had the happiest of evenings with them, I hardly slept that night, overwhelmed by the wretched blackness. Strange. Insomnia had never been a problem.

Another incident was uncharacteristic. We spent a lunch hour with a couple at Regent College, Vancouver, and enjoyed sandwiches with them in the foyer, beside a large bookshop. 'You must have a good browse, Elaine!' our friends insisted. 'You'll love it in there!' So I went to scan the shelves but my usual eagerness for books had gone. I couldn't get enthused, and felt sorry that I must be disappointing our kind friends. In the end the husband bought a book and presented it to me. I was very touched by his thoughtfulness. It helped me to feel better.

The middle week of the holiday was spent with our son, Stuart, in Connecticut where the autumn colours of New England were approaching their full glory. So good to catch up on news and to share outings together! I managed to keep up with the itinerary and enjoyed many a meal out, though never managed much more than a side salad and an ice cream. (Americans offer big helpings!) One morning Stuart took us to another bookshop, even larger than the one at Regent, and pointed out the cafe in one corner. 'You're supposed to choose a pile of books, then go and browse through them over coffee. No particular obligation to buy,' Stuart explained. I soon found a small daily reading book which included personal stories, so took it to the coffee shop. There, at a table on my own, I lingered over a few pages and, in doing so, felt deeply refreshed. It was a quiet oasis of peace in the midst of our holiday, and I sensed that it had been carefully planned by God.

The final week of the trip was spent on the Gulf coast of Florida where my sister had offered us her holiday flat. The tropical loveliness of the extensive grounds around the flat complex immediately delighted me, being a happy reminder of childhood years in Kenya. Those last few days on our own brought special pleasure! – a boat trip to see alligators in a shallow lake, visits to the beach, an aquarium, a wild life park. And then, as darkness fell at the end of each day, a leisurely meal on the verandah, watching distant storms light up the sky. I mostly forgot about my problems. What a relief to feel cheerful and well! Maybe the holiday had brought about the physical and mental cure for which I so much longed? But the doctor had warned this was unlikely to happen, and whenever I thought about returning home I knew it wasn't an empty warning. Deep down I was afraid of going back to the place which was now associated with so much disappointment and frustration. How strange I should feel this way. Always before it had been a pleasure to return after a holiday. Our last day in Florida came, and we faced the long flight back. How would I cope with all the inevitable unpacking, sorting out, catching up as soon as we opened the front door? 'Please help me, Lord' I prayed many times during the overnight journey. The request was certainly heard and answered for, to my surprise, I managed, with ease, to get everything shipshape within a day of our return. That was reassuring!

5. FEW LIGHTS IN THIS TUNNEL

What was I going to do with the autumn weeks ahead? One part of me longed to be involved again with activities in the community and church, but mostly I felt overwhelmed at such a prospect. I was finding it hard enough to cope at home. But there was Good Morning Group, the Tuesday Bible discussion time for ladies, at the Church Hall. It was good to continue to be there every week, to introduce each morning, and sometimes to lead the study. Admittedly I was anxious beforehand, wondering if I would manage to be calm and collected, but once surrounded by my friends fears eased and I was able to keep going. Afterwards I felt spent and needed the afternoon to sleep and recover, but it was worth it. Good Morning Group was important to me, and I valued the help of a particular friend who was there praying quietly for me every Tuesday morning. Ironically, our Autumn studies were based on Hebrews chapter 11, the 'people of great faith' chapter, and I felt ashamed about my own lack of faith and resultant anxiety. Such guilt feelings were unhelpful, though, and in time I came to accept the doctor's insistence that the hyper-anxiety was yet another aspect of the depressive illness. God knew that I was an unwilling, helpless victim to it, and felt only understanding and compassion towards me. What a relief when I let this sink in! Words I had read recently were so true:

It is a kind of blasphemy to view ourselves with so little compassion when God views us with so much
(Michael Mayne, 'This Sunrise of Wonder').

As the studies in Hebrews continued I began, instead, to be encouraged by the people of faith the chapter portrays. After all, they were human like everyone else and, since one verse (34) says that they 'won strength out of weakness' it would seem that they, too, experienced times of understandable anxiety. Their subsequent faith came entirely as a gift from God; it was not natural to them. So couldn't God give faith to me, as well? That was a positive request with which to counteract earlier negative guilt and, as the last part of the chapter shows, God gives faith to suffer as well as to overcome. Yes, in the end, Hebrews 11 led to a great deal of helpful discovery. My small faith began to reach out and hold on more tightly to God and, in doing so, was strengthened a little.

While Good Morning Group was my main ongoing area of responsibility I did still manage to help in small ways at church – reading the lesson, helping with the creche, collating the monthly magazine. Each was important to me, showing that I was not entirely 'set aside'. About this time I heard of a need for someone to help once a month at the Baby Clinic in the village. Despite hesitancy about taking on anything else – and the doctor's advice not to do so – this idea strongly appealed and I offered to fill the gap. Over the months it has become one of the best afternoons in the month. Not that I do anything more than find each baby's card and sell milk powder when needed. But it gives an opportunity to spend time with a new group of people – little ones and mums – and it has further helped to take me beyond my problems.

How important, yet hard, it was to be willing to move out beyond my adversity. Despite knowing my need to be involved with a few activities I sometimes found this involvement increasingly difficult and there were days when I wanted to stay quietly at home and do nothing at all. (This was very uncharacteristic. I've always loved to be up and doing.) On one such morning, when I woke wishing the Teasmade wasn't about to launch me into another day, Les commented, 'You're pitying yourself, you know.' It was painful to hear those words, since I'd been trying hard to steer clear of self-pity, but I knew he was right. 'I feel bad about those thoughts,' I admitted later, unable to get Les' words out of my mind. He looked gently at me. 'Don't feel bad. It's all part of this depressive illness,' he explained. 'Those thoughts will go.' I was grateful that he had been frank about the self-pity. It was excusable maybe, but I must fight it.

Always before I had experienced dark 'patches', now the darkness began to last all day. At first there were only a couple of such days a week, but gradually the proportion changed. It was like being sucked into a dark tunnel with few lights. The doctor noted this trend when I went for the usual fortnightly check-up. Physically I was doing better, however, and this fact was a most welcome light in the darkness.

Maybe I didn't need the anti-nausea tablets anymore? Les was sure they were contributing to the depression and, when the doctor checked on this, the drug notes stated that such an affliction could be a side-effect, so I was advised to stop them immediately. I remember that morning clearly. It was a brilliant sunlit day in late autumn, and as we came in through the front door the hall walls were alight with dozens of small rainbows, each reflected from a crystal butterfly attached to the window. I gazed at their bright colours and remembered the Bible promise of hope, symbolized in the rainbow. Yes, now that I had stopped the drug there was a strong new shaft of hope. 'It will take about three weeks to make a difference,' the doctor had said. I couldn't wait for those three weeks to pass. Once home Les made mugs of coffee and as we sat sipping them we stopped to give thanks to God for what could well provide the longed-for breakthrough. To celebrate I took the trouble to make savoury mince for lunch, using fresh meat, for once, instead of opening a tin. To anyone else that would have seemed insignificant, but to me it was an important step forward. Maybe my desire to cook would soon return?

Not that I'd given up in the kitchen altogether. Soup-making was simple but gave pleasure and satisfaction. That day I prepared a big pan of broth and later, when we set out for an early-evening drive, I delivered a bowl of it to an elderly friend nearby.

'I've something for you too!' he announced and presented me with a small Begonia Rex which he had raised from a parent plant. What colourful, silvered leaves! 'I'll enjoy raising that further!' I thought happily as we drove along. The last light of the bright, sunlit day was fading but the autumn colours still glowed a soft gold. It had been a good day, full of new hope.

*****

On a Monday afternoon soon afterwards, I helped at the occasional Tea held for elderly patients from a psychiatric hospital. I've been doing this for years but this time felt an unexpected deeper bond with our friends. It was possible to feel something of their frustration, rather than merely observe from the outside. I was surprised yet pleased. The patients love music and on this occasion the entertainment was given by a singer and pianist. Their choice of light pieces, and a medley of Scottish tunes was just right for the patients. And, listening and watching, I was unexpectedly refreshed too. It was fun and I was glad that it was still possible to enter into such pleasure, even though the disturbing darkness was increasing.

Why? Surely it would ease now that I was no longer taking those pills? Each day I looked for the first signs of improvement, convinced they would soon be apparent. But they weren't and I tried desperately to cover the disappointment. Instead two unwelcome things happened. The sleepiness went, and so did any desire to eat.

One night, as we snuggled down in bed, I tried to tell Les about the increased darkness and the irrational fears which were a part of it. Afterwards I felt concerned that I had burdened him. This whole horrible experience was bad enough for Les without me detailing it. 'Sorry to be such a moaner,' I apologized, but he merely offered a comforting hug, and I was soon asleep. But not for long. Insomnia had become a frequent problem now. I was suddenly wide awake again and tried to counteract those wretched nameless fears with thoughts of the past – childhood, nursing training, mission work abroad. It didn't help. The early morning hours dragged. I couldn't understand what was happening. All my life I'd slept with ease, now it was so different. The blackness and fear closed in on me. I was desperate, but found some relief in simply repeating 'Jesus' over and over again in the silence of my heart ... and at last morning came.

That was one of many more such nights and, since I couldn't sleep after lunch now either, I soon grew very tired. One day I came across words on a card and tried to remember them as I went up to bed that evening:

I will not lie down with evil,
Nor shall evil lie down with me.
But I will lie down with God,
And God will lie down with me
                    (Hebridean Celtic Prayers and
                         Songs – Carmina Gadelica).

39

The verse helped me to see that I was not lying down with evil, however powerful the darkness seemed. God, in Jesus, was still there to protect and keep me, for he had promised, 'I will never leave you; I will never abandon you' (Hebrews 13:5, GNB). Those words could provide a strong beam of light to me in the darkness.

*****

Jesus so lovingly touches our lives through the thoughtfulness of others, and at exactly the right moment too. One evening when I was feeling particularly low a friend called unexpectedly, bringing a posy of flowers. A lovely sight in dark November! My friend pulled a chair up by the fireside and sat with me, asking exactly the right questions and making exactly the right comments. She was struggling with a depressive illness herself, and could relate closely to my situation. She fully understood; we spoke the same language. How much this meant! I didn't have to struggle to explain myself.

That was the start of an important, deepening bond with this friend, which I continue to value. Often when we see each other we will enquire, 'What sort of week have you had?' 'How's today going for you?' Both of us know what we are talking about and can answer in honest terms instead of giving the customary, often false, reply – 'Fine thanks!'

The gift of flowers that evening was specially appreciated. I love flowers and had received so many during the acute earlier stage of my physical illness. Now it was a friend who herself knew deep mental distress who thought to bring me that colourful posy and, when arranging the blooms, I realized that people are only too ready to give flowers to the physically sick, but don't often take them to a depressed person. I used to be like that as well but have since found that flowers are, perhaps, even more appreciated when your mind and emotions are in turmoil. They offer peace and loveliness, perfection and order, and that is therapeutic. I love to gaze at flowers! They help to bring calm. In fact, just after my friend's thoughtful gift a very large bouquet arrived from our son in America. How exquisite those many different mauve and pink flowers were! – lilies, carnations, chrysanthemums, and several more. Even my largest vase couldn't contain them so I had to borrow a huge one from a neighbour. The bouquet lasted for more than a month and cheered me over and over again – when I was open to being cheered.

It was much harder now to be open. The inner darkness, with its nameless fears, troubled me throughout each day as well as during those long, distressing hours before dawn. There were only a few brief patches of lightness and ease. I could feel the depression like a heavy weight, pressing hard against my brain. Every earlier symptom had become much worse. I struggled to keep functional in the kitchen, even though recipe failures were now more common and any pleasure in cooking had completely gone. Decision-making became hard in the extreme, and I would dither in shops, or over the simplest choices at home. Should I write that letter, or call in on a lonely neighbour instead? Should I cycle to the village shops, or take the car? Should I make a supper date with friends, or would it be better simply to invite them for coffee? Concentration on reading and listening became poor, and I found it hard to follow a more involved conversation for long. Also, people who were talkative tired me out. I just couldn't cope, even though that had never been a problem before. I had enjoyed being a listener, now talkativeness made me impatient, even agitated. Everything, whether decision-making, routine work around the home, listening to others, or a visit to the local shops required enormous willpower and effort. This was all so strange to me, and the more these difficulties increased, the more distressed I became. Not that I expressed the distress in words or weeping. No, it was better to keep it inside I decided, especially for Les' sake. Only occasionally did I give him a peep beneath the surface. But, being a perceptive person, he sensed much more than I was prepared to reveal.

One morning I went to a friend's house for our occasional one-to-one Bible study, and it was good to relax in her home and catch up on news of the family. As I left we lingered on the doorstep chatting, and my friend suddenly asked, 'How are you?' I could see that she was wondering what was up (did it show now?) and so, briefly, I explained that I'd been feeling down for a while, but hoped soon to be on the up-and-up. My friend looked out over her

November garden, then said, 'I think these low times are like winter, very hard and long. Sometimes you wonder if it will ever end. But there is going to be a springtime, and even now all those lovely spring plants are developing deep down under the soil. They're already getting ready!' We gave each other a warm hug and, as I came home, her words kept going through my mind. Yes, there will be a springtime in my life! But meanwhile I had to struggle with the 'now'. What was happening to me? How low was I going to get? Would it result in admission to hospital? Sometimes, in my desperation even that prospect seemed welcome. In such a setting, I would be able to relax, knowing that everyone understood. Later I was shocked that a hospital ward had been a welcome prospect. How could I have felt like that? It only showed how serious the depressive illness had become.

6. WINTER IS A LONG JOURNEY

Faith is weakness hanging on to strength
(Festo Kivengere).

Winter was approaching. The first snow fell in mid-November; huge ragged flakes which whitened the ground but melted later in the weak sunshine. The beech trees on the far river bank were now quite bare, but a single poplar tree insisted on clutching at its last few leaves. One morning we saw a doe running through the field beyond the trees, and a few days later a mink scampered along the river bank. Many mornings I would hear the strange, mournful cry of wild geese as, flock upon arrowed flock, they flew overhead towards their feeding grounds, only to return at sunset to roost at a nearby loch.

Winter. An extra hard time when you are struggling with depression. The battle in my mind had now intensified, evident on various fronts. One was the temptation to self-pity. It had constantly to be fought. I would tell myself to think about 'all those people facing terrible suffering in Bosnia, or Rwanda, or Afghanistan'. But such tactics weren't helpful. Yes, their need was far greater, but setting it alongside my own adversity merely made me feel guilty about being in my condition at all. And such guilt, I was discovering, is not only unhelpful, but inappropriate. 'Remember that you are ill,' the doctor had insisted. 'Just as much as if you had pneumonia or appendicitis.'

Another battle was with envy. Envy of a most strange kind, such as I had never known before. I felt envious of a friend, now on holiday in Florida, and of a couple who were in Malta for two weeks. What a great time they'd all be having! I wanted to be away on holiday too, enjoying all that fun. But in better moments I knew this was sheer escapism, nor would I find a holiday enjoyable in my present state of mind. Hadn't the Canada/USA trip been tough at times? Worse still, I began to envy the physically ill. 'If only I had an obvious physical illness like them and could refer to it freely, knowing I'd be understood,' I'd think to myself. But for me it was all so different. A friend had been suddenly threatened with the loss of her hearing, another was in hospital with disturbing symptoms. And to think that I envied the rightful sympathy both were being given. That seemed so wrong but, in fact, it was yet another symptom of this wretched inner turmoil. The reasoning part of my mind was incapable of normal function.

Hence the irrational fears. They were so hard to put into words. Only those who have experienced depression could fully understand. What *was* I afraid of? Fear of incompetence when driving the car, fear of not being able to give good leadership at the Tuesday Good Morning Group, fear of being lost for the right words when in company, fear of being alone for any length of time, and so on. And then the worst fear of all – that I was losing my mind. I could not reason myself out of these fears, nor could anyone else. And as the fears grew so self-confidence diminished still further.

For much of the time fear also took the form of foreboding. Foreboding of what? I didn't know. I only feared that something awful was going to happen to a close friend, or a relative. What? When? How? Again, I didn't know. This foreboding would weigh heavily on my mind and intensify to overwhelming proportions during the long, sleepless hours of the night.

Fear. Fear. Fear. There seemed to be no escape, no chance of winning the battle. After long onslaughts I was left exhausted and deeply troubled. But no one really knew, because I could not put it into words, nor did I want to. Except into prayer words.

I poured out my despair to God, pleading for immediate relief and healing. But despite asking over and over again relief didn't come. Was I expecting it enough? I didn't know. My mind was too muddled. But I did begin, very tentatively, to consider one possibility. It resulted from reading about a desperate sufferer whose persistent plea was also 'Lord, heal me' until he realized there was a more important request – 'Lord, to what purpose is this illness?' Gradually I recognized that everything in our lives has God-given purpose and that we can only begin to come to terms with suffering when we open ourselves to discovering what that purpose is. An understanding friend emphasised this in a letter she sent:

'I had been through a particularly difficult time and had really come to the end of my tether, although I still trusted God's word and clung desperately to it. One day, when I was reading Ezekiel God spoke to me very definitely through chapter 14 verse 23. "And ye shall know that I have not done without cause all that I have done." I was so encouraged to remember that the Lord does care about what happens to us, and even in our deepest darkness and confusion we can know that he has a reason for allowing us to go through this dark time.'

About the same time another friend wrote out some insights gained from reading Ronald Dunn's book *When Heaven is Silent* and gave them to me:

'God never explains why. Our response must be to every inexplicable trial "What now?" This not only saves us from self pity but it gives us something to look forward to. "What now?" means we are still moving, still growing. In short we have a future. It means that life can be good again.'

She concluded with a quotation from the book:

'Faith is not necessarily the power to make things the way we want them to be, it is the courage to face things as they are. The very thing I am wrestling with may be the thing God wants to use to bless me.'

Could God bless me in the midst of this turmoil? It was important to give the matter careful thought, so I decided to try and trace the different ways in which he *was* giving purpose to this trial, and in doing so blessing me.

I soon recognized that God's prime purpose was to deepen my love/trust relationship with him, through Jesus. In my acute need I'd reached out to him again and again and in doing so had begun to experience new depths of his love and compassion. God was there for me, in Jesus. I could come to him at any time, night or day. I was not alone, not forgotten. Furthermore, God totally understood my condition and empathised deeply with me. No one else could do this. Ours was a unique relationship. As I pondered this, and the way in which it could help to ease my fear and foreboding, God brought some Bible words to my mind:

> 'God loves you, so don't let anything worry you or frighten you' (Daniel 10:19, GNB).

What strong comfort that statement gave! And it still does. I am wrapped around with the love of God. Safely sheltered. All will ultimately be well. Can I hold onto that? 'Faith is weakness hanging on to strength.' I also came to recognize that my love for Jesus was growing in the midst of this trial, simply because I needed him so much. Utter dependence is humbling, but at the same time immensely enriching.

Another important purpose in God's allowing of

adversity was that I might be able to understand and empathize with others. I had never known the intense suffering a depressive illness can cause. Before I had been sympathetic, though held certain reservations. 'How could he/she have got into such a state? Where is their Christian faith? Surely it isn't as bad as they're making out?' These had been my reactions and each served to show how little I knew, and how shallow was my sympathy. Now God had allowed me to discover some of the depths of depression. It was a most salutary learning. I thought back to friends who had once travelled a similar hard path. A missionary, a teacher, a student, a scientist, a busy mum. Now I knew what it had been like for them. And such a knowing was important, particularly when I considered friends who were at present in the midst of such a struggle. Seven came to mind and I realized that the empathy I now felt needed to be expressed in a brief letter, a phone call, a visit, maybe a small gift. But most of all I could pray for them, one on each day of the week. This has since become important, deepening love for the people concerned. The bond of suffering is strong and deep, and very valuable.

There was yet another purpose to be acknowledged and implemented. That of learning to 'be' rather than to insist on 'doing'. Over the months I had been so determined to fight the depression, and also to put some sort of value into each day, that I had driven myself to over-activity when it came to visiting people, or helping out within the community and church. Although limitations had been recognized I had nonetheless overstretched myself, against the doctor's wise advice. Far from easing the condition this had only served to intensify the stress. Now, in my desperation, I was more ready to acknowledge that God didn't want all my 'doings'. First and foremost he waited for me to be still before him, able to relax a little and enjoy him for himself alone. And if it took weakness and illness to bring me to that point, so be it.

One morning, when the weak November sun shone out across the hills, I decided to take a 'be still' walk with Jesus along a forest path, not far from home. It was good to feel the keen breeze on my face, and to hear it sighing through the tall pines. I began to feel refreshed, my mind a little eased. The path was carpeted with crisp brown leaves and, as I strolled along, I felt Jesus' walking with me, enjoying my enjoyment. It was so good to be quietly with him! During that time together I was also able to face and confess sins that needed forgiveness and removal. Such a relief! Later, back in the car, I sat and gazed at the far hills, calmed, comforted and full of gratitude. That morning of 'being' helped me to rediscover peace, at least for a little while. Would I also ease off on the 'doing' from now on? In an attempt to do so I cut down on my programme, putting only a couple of goals into each day, so that there would still be a sense of purpose. That remained important.

*****

One of the hardest aspects of a depressive illness is that a positive mindset can't be maintained. Just when you think you're on the way up at last you're dragged down by a really bad day, or a disturbing development. As November progressed and the days shortened I found that the evenings became difficult. I was tired, and had little inclination to read or listen to music. At such times it was hard to keep despair at bay. 'I think we should get a television set,' Les suggested. Due to spending much of our married life abroad in third world countries where television was not an option, we had found other ways of relaxing at the end of the day. But now the idea held tentative appeal and we decided to try it out. I knew a television would make things easier for Les, who had reached the point of foregoing some evening activities, in order to stay home and keep me company. The despair was always worse if I was alone. Les' suggestion was a success, and although we only watched for about an hour each evening, it helped to distract my mind and offered an interesting wider window on the world. For some reason comedy programmes didn't appeal to me at all and even Les' much-loved cartoons failed to raise my usual laugh. My sense of humour had been considerably impaired and I hadn't quite realized that until the TV moved into our house. About this time we also began to play Scrabble a few evenings a week; very good exercise for my sluggish brain.

Weekends had now become difficult as well, particularly Saturdays. On Sunday there was more to do, with morning and evening services at church and maybe a walk or drive in the afternoon. But Saturdays lacked the usual weekday routine and as a result seemed purposeless and empty. I began to fill them with over-activity (back to all that 'doing' again) but that wasn't an answer. I merely ended up weary and discouraged. Instead we decided to make Saturdays special by going out for a 'car picnic' to a popular viewpoint, or by taking a scenic route along the River Dee. Sometimes we called on friends, or had lunch at a favourite restaurant. It was a happy challenge to think up a Saturday plan as the week ended and such activities certainly eased the weekend blues. This plan also demanded flexibility as, until Friday night, we never quite knew how our Saturday would be spent.

Flexibility. I was finding that difficult in other contexts, especially when any long-planned event suddenly had to be cancelled. That happened when I invited a city friend to lunch and spent a great deal of time fussing over the menu, aware that my friend was a competent cook. The day before our date I shopped and baked and had everything ready when, to my dismay, a heavy overnight fall of snow meant that the visit had to be cancelled. In my tense condition I found that strangely hard to take. The day seemed to have fallen apart and now I had nothing to do. (I dreaded having nothing to do, empty days always being darkest of all.) Les sensed my sudden bewilderment. 'Let's make another plan,' he suggested, and he helped me to put the day together again. Snow or no snow, we went to the village shop for coffee, visited an elderly housebound friend, and then set off to the nearest town for supermarket groceries. By the end of the afternoon I felt much better. By then God's wise instruction in Psalm 46:10 had begun to go through my mind – 'Be still, and know that I am God' – and I tried to let him still me once again.

It became important on many later occasions to try and let God still me, especially when agitated; another feature of the depressive illness. After being out for a while at a friend's house, or at an evening event, I would desperately want to get home, and become inwardly agitated until it was possible to leave. Unexpected delays also induced a similar response and I remember sitting in a restaurant where the service was extremely slow, and getting so worked up inside that my enjoyment of the meal was considerably lessened. Again, this agitation was very uncharacteristic and caused much distress. Perhaps it was due to the insecurity which is part of the depressive illness? At such times I tried hard to let Jesus calm me and felt a measure of relief when I thought of the shepherd figure in our bedroom at home. Jesus, the Good Shepherd, was closely with me. Perhaps even carrying me? I could 'coorie' (nestle) into him, as a local friend once put it.

*****

Every November I aim to complete Christmas shopping early, and then stay well clear of the busy city until the new year. And so, despite continued physical weakness and my depressive condition, I decided to do the same again this time. Les warned me against it – 'You just won't cope' – but I was determined to select personal gifts rather than, as he suggested, to order everything from a catalogue. The day was carefully planned, with the shops to be visited numbered from 1 to 10 on my list, according to their location in the city. 'That's far too much!' Les responded, but I set out nonetheless. I had not taken my decision-making problem into account at all and came unstuck at the very first shop; a bookstore where I planned to buy four gifts. *Could* I decide what books to buy and for whom? It was a major challenge and I flitted from one shelf to the next in growing anxiety. Eventually I found fairly suitable books and hurried away to shop no.2. A whole hour had already passed. By midday I was spent, with 7 more stops to go. Agitation set in, so I took a couple of bought sandwiches all the way back to the car, and sat very still for a while gazing at the nearby park. Why such difficulty? Hadn't I always coped fine with a Christmas challenge like this? Was I losing my mind? I ate the snack slowly and sadly, leaning back into the seat as if leaning back against God. In time I felt a little better and made a new plan – to drive to a car park nearer the rest of the chosen shops, and to get through the remainder of the list as calmly as possible. It worked and, at last, I headed for home. But the experience greatly unnerved me and a few dark days of frustration followed. Couldn't I even handle a city shopping trip now? The doctor was right. 'Don't attempt more than you can manage. The resulting failure will only set you back.' I'd had to learn the hard way – again.

It was after this, afraid that my mind really *was* going, that I asked my two prayer partners if they could come round and lay hands on my head. How much I valued their doing so, and what a sense of peace and reassurance came after that time of prayer and specific commitment of the problem to God. It was also a relief to pour out some of my inner feelings and fears and to feel their power over me thus being broken. Both my friends gave me a warm hug before they set off for home which greatly helped to reassure and affirm me. I may have been struggling with a muddled, troubled mind but I still mattered to them. How much it meant to know this!

Did I expect an immediate return to normal mental function? Immediate relief from the depressive illness? Part of me did believe for this, but I also knew that, in wisdom, God might yet have further humbling experiences ahead. Valuable learnings, each working together for good in my life, and important for the future. I needed to acknowledge both alternatives and, whatever the outcome, to reach out and hold on more tightly to God.

One morning, a few days later, I found myself singing a hymn as I vacuumed the stairs. Instead of merely repeating familiar words I stopped to think about them as I worked...

How sweet the name of Jesus sounds
    In a believer's ear!
It soothes his sorrows, heals his wounds,
    And drives away his fear.

It makes the wounded spirit whole,
    And calms the troubled breast;
'Tis manna to the hungry soul,
    And to the weary rest.

The words lingered in my mind, a welcome oasis in the middle of the morning, which strengthened me. How careful Jesus is to meet us with just the right words at the right moment! The same happened again when, later that week, a friend in whom I had confided sent me a card:

'My prayers are for you at the start of this new day. At present the light outside is covered by a typical November mist and damp, but as the hours pass so the sun will rise and, although it may not break through the cloud, nevertheless it will bring us light.

'I pray that in your darkness you may feel and know that the light and warmth of God's Son is with you and will break through your hours of darkness. It is good that in days of darkness we can walk in the light of the Lord.'

I tried to rest my mind more in these strong truths and peace came, at least for a while. Then it was unexpectedly shattered. We had been invited to a theatre production in the city and, for some reason, the title made me think it was a musical. 'Just right as a light hearted pre-Christmas treat!' I thought and we set out eagerly with a couple of friends. But the production was not a musical and was very far from being light hearted. Before the first ten minutes had passed I began to feel uneasy about the strange, sinister atmosphere of the play, and the uneasiness grew until I had to shut my eyes at the worst places. However would I manage to stay until the end? I worried, my mind becoming more and more distressed. At the interval our friends chatted away happily but Les also felt concerned about the play. 'If we weren't responsible for the transport home I'd leave now,' he said. Somehow we saw the production through – it was a little easier in the second half – but the evening had greatly disturbed me. I couldn't get the sights, scenes and sound effects out of my mind and spent the next couple of days trying hard to regain my equilibrium. I needed the hymn words even more then. God must have deliberately given me those verses in advance, aware that I would particularly need them after that evening out. His timing is exactly right!

*****

It was time for another check-up with the doctor. By now I was desperate about the ongoing insomnia and the frightening inner darkness experienced during those sleepless nights. 'I think we should start you on anti-depressants,' the doctor suggested. 'But the decision is up to you.' I was only too glad to know that the condition could be eased, and was not reluctant at all. Nor did I feel ashamed that, as a Christian, I was in need of such medication. Wasn't this another way in which God could work together for good in my life? So I accepted the prescription slip gratefully. 'The effect won't be noticeable for about three weeks,' I was warned, 'and then only in gradual ways. But you *will* sleep better right from tonight!' What a relief! And that's exactly what happened. I enjoyed a long, deep sleep that night, and have done so ever since. It has also meant that, at last, I can put my troubled mind to sleep. It wakes up much the better for such a rest.

*****

The understanding friend who had visited earlier on with flowers slipped something into my hand at church one Sunday – a small cross-stitched marker which read 'When things are down look up'. I liked that, and realized how privileged we are to be able to look up to God, who is tenderly there for us. But I thought also of another friend who, in their acute depression, felt abandoned, as if God was 'a million miles away'. This concerned me. God's nearness, in Jesus, had been crucial to me all along. I could not bear to think of him withdrawing. One afternoon, when resting on the settee, I said quite simply to Jesus, 'I'm so afraid that you will one day abandon me.' Immediately I sensed his quiet, significant answer: 'No, don't be anxious. On the cross I experienced abandonment on your behalf so that it would never happen to you.' What strong reassurance! The fear was silenced. I thought again of my troubled friend and realized that though, in his condition, he felt abandoned, it was not actually so. Hadn't the Lord promised, 'I will not fail you or forsake you' (Joshua 1:5 RSV,)? And we could trust him to keep his promises.

I realized, too, that sometimes this sense of abandonment triggers anger at God, as can the very fact of being the victim of a depressive illness. 'God, why have you let this happen to me? Why aren't you there to do something about it?' Such indignation is understandable, another manifestation of the condition itself. Though spared such anger, I can see how easily it would be aroused, and it is also important for people to know that, in fact, God has not abandoned them, nor does he stand accusingly over those struggling with such strong feelings. He understands, taking our vulnerability into full consideration. To go on a guilt trip regarding one's anger would be inappropriate.

Thinking of guilt trips, I found that this was becoming a problem; guilt over being so anxious, impatient and agitated. I knew they were all part of the condition but that didn't cure the guilt trip tendency. One evening I asked Les, 'Should I feel guilty about all these things?' 'The answer hinges on what you do with the impatience and worry,' he said. 'If you wallow in guilt that's wrong, but if you turn to God and ask him to help you overcome these difficulties he will, even if it takes time. So then there's no place for guilt. He sees your heart's intention. That's what matters.' Les' answer certainly helped to set my mind at rest.

*****

December came. There were good things ahead! The month was greeted by a spectacular flypast of 17 whooper swans early one morning. What a sight! These wintering birds give us much pleasure and we miss them when they fly north to the Arctic for summer breeding.

Our daughter, Rachel, arrived for a few days early in December. How good to see her, and to enjoy mother-and-daughter chats and outings. We lingered long in a couple of favourite coffee shops, catching up on one another. Knowing my difficulties, Rachel had come to help me get ready for Christmas so all my gifts were soon wrapped, and she took care of numerous other bits and pieces. That cheered me, and simply having Rachel with us brought fun and laughter to our home. So good! It was sad to see her off on the train at midday on the Sunday but afterwards we made the occasion happier by taking a car picnic down to the beach. That's a favourite place. We both love to watch the ships ply in and out of the nearby harbour while we sit and eat our sandwiches.

Another good aspect of December was the fact that Christmas mail began to arrive from friends worldwide. I spent a long time each day studying the cards and reading everyone's news. It enabled me to enter into other situations and took me far away from my own bewildering circumstances. That was very therapeutic! It seemed that this year the words 'love' 'joy' and 'peace' featured more often on the cards and I tried to hold on to them, and to the wonder and simplicity of the Christmas story.

It was also good to be now experiencing some benefit from the anti-depressant medication – a slight easing of the irrational fear and anxiety. And although I had to admit that the days were still somewhat dark, lighter patches had started to break through. The frightening downward trend had certainly been arrested. Would it be all 'up' from now on? I deeply longed for steady improvement. So did Les. He shared my encouragement at each sign of progress. Physically I was not so well but that didn't trouble me unduly. Physical complaints were so much easier to bear. The nausea had returned, and some pain, but I felt sure they would ease off in due course.

Sometimes I still pondered the comment 'I never thought this would happen to me' and realized how careful we need to be not to think of ourselves as being immune or above certain problems. They come to anyone, anytime. A salutary, humbling fact which should elicit sympathy from others rather than criticism. I wondered if people knew of my condition and tended to criticise, secretly in their hearts if not openly? 'Fancy *her* getting that!' A close friend told me that many in the village were now aware of my problem. How did that make me feel? Thinking this over I found that I was glad because that would reveal how frail and vulnerable I was, how needy. The whole experience had shown these facts up and, in the process, I had been brought very low.

Les had an additional comment to offer when we were chatting over tea soon afterwards. 'It's interesting that, as in Job's case, adversity may well have its ultimate origin in heaven. God is allowing Satan to harass us, but others only see a person's depression and tend to be shocked and to blame them, as with Job's comforters. The truth is very different. There's an all-important heavenly factor. God is allowing this testing of someone whom he greatly loves and values.' Yes, I needed to remember that too. There is so much to discover in the midst of a hard, long journey!

*****

With all this thinking I had to be careful not to become too self-focused, a tendency that had to be fought all along. So, whether feeling physically fit or not, I still planned a visit to a friend each day, and also programmed in other 'help others' things. They were small and insignificant, but therapeutic to me. Exercise was another help and, weather permitting, I continued to cycle to the shops. It was good to chat with others in the High Street, and also to buy fresh food most days and to make myself prepare meals without resorting to tins and packets. But when I felt queasy that was hard. Nonetheless I was determined. I must keep going on this upward trend!

Christmas came and went. Quiet, happy and simple, with our two sons here for a couple of nights. It was fun to have lunch out on Christmas Eve, and I even accepted an invitation to a party a few days later, though I didn't manage to see the whole evening out. I still became agitated if away from home for long, and being in the company of numerous jolly people dismayed me a bit too. I could only take such an atmosphere in small doses.

Over the Christmas holiday I arranged two small lunch parties at home, choosing simple yet tasty menus. It was fun and I loved having four or five extra people around the mealtable. After each occasion I felt cheered by the company, and glad that I had made the effort. Yes, December had been a good month and there were even a few whole days of peace and ease when the darkness was ousted altogether.

About this time a friend sent me a poem which further brought hope as the new year approached:

I love a tree,
A brave, upstanding tree!
When I am wearied in the strife,
Beaten by storms and bruised by life,
I look up at a tree, and it refreshes me.
If it can keep its head held high
And look the storm straight in the eye,
Ready to stand, ready to die,
Then by the grace of God can I –
At least with Heaven's help I'll try;
I love a tree, for it refreshes me.

I love a tree!
When it seems dead,
Its leaves all shorn and bared its head,
When winter flings its cold and snow,
It stands there undismayed by woe;
It stands there waiting for the spring –
A tree is such a believing thing.
I love a tree,
For it refreshes me!

(Ralph Spalding Cushman.
From 'Hilltop Verses and Prayers.')

7. ON TOWARDS THE SUNLIGHT

Winter struck when January came, but the snow was not without its beauty. One morning the temperature was -18 degrees, despite bright sunlight, and when I looked out of the window the trees were sheathed in ice, as if decked with gleaming jewels. Magnificent! Later I set out along the riverside path and came across a wide expanse of pure, shining, unspoiled snow, so I turned from the grubby well-trodden track to walk right across such beckoning newness. It was fun, and also a parable perhaps? A whole new unlived year beckoned too!

On December 31st, I made a last entry in my note-book and then ruled a line right across the bottom of the page. At last I could leave the difficult year behind and set off with eagerness into what lay ahead. Paul's words came to mind: '...one thing I do, forgetting what lies behind and straining forward to what lies ahead, I press on toward the goal...' (Philippians 3:13, 14, RSV).

It was so good to be full of new expectation, boosted still further by the fact that I now experienced all good days with some bad patches rather than all bad days with some good patches. I was keen to tell the doctor on one of my now less frequent visits. The nausea had improved so I didn't mention it.

We made one Sunday extra-special by inviting a family round to lunch and I prepared a simple meal – melon with grapes, beef and dumpling casserole served with the last of the garden parsnips, and then a chocolate trifle. Everyone was appreciative and the success of the occasion helped to restore self-confidence.

When settling down to sleep that night I realized that I no longer yearned for bed in order to have a distressed mind switched off. Now I went to bed with a quite normal eagerness and it continued to be a blessing to sleep so well, even if this was induced by medication.

*****

Over the months I had become very dependent upon Les which, in many ways, was inevitable. My suffering had often been his suffering but I had not realized how much he felt it. Now I sensed a need to consider him and his needs much more, to talk about his printing work, his flying interests, his thoughts for the long-term future, etc. We had many a good chat around the fireside. How much I valued Les for his acceptance of me despite my condition; his straightforwardness and clearcut insights, his availability. And even his genuine appreciation of the meals I put together. One day, after serving him reheated turkey, followed by a bowl of banana custard he said, 'That was very nice!' And meant it! Little did Les know what he was letting himself in for when on our wedding day he promised to keep me 'in sickness and in health'. But he has been utterly loyal and supportive through it all.

My desire to consider Les and his concerns was rather undermined, however, one day in early January when he invited me to join him on a trip to collect a piece of printing equipment. I was wary as past experience had taught me that when Les met up with a printing expert he would chat at great length, sounding out his friend on numerous aspects of the job. Once I'd spent two and a half hours in a strange sittingroom, while Les talked printing out in the workshop. Les noticed my wariness this time. 'Don't worry,' he responded. 'This chap's bound to be working and he won't want to spare me more than ten minutes, so we can have a quick turnaround and then a picnic lunch on the way home.' With this reassurance I agreed and we set off happily together. But the printer wasn't busy, in fact he was only too glad to meet up with a like-minded fellow on his slack day. It took ages for him to produce the item we'd come to collect and then much more time to show Les round his extensive workshop. As the two of them set various machines in motion and talked on and on about their work I became bored, then agitated, and finally so upset that I couldn't stop myself touching Les' arm in an unspoken plea. The printer saw and immediately responded, 'Oh, you're bored, aren't you.' It seemed like a rebuke and I regretted my action, but it was almost midday and I didn't know how much longer I'd be stuck in that cold workplace. Les broke off his eager chat and we left soon afterwards, but the country picnic which followed was overshadowed by sadness and guilt.

Les had so little opportunity to talk printing and I'd interrupted this rare pleasure. He told me he didn't really mind, but I knew he did. It was a difficult day.

*****

Good Morning Group was in full swing again after the Christmas break and we summed up the studies in Hebrews 11 by looking at the first verses of chapter 12:

> '...let us also lay aside every weight...and let us run with perseverance the race that is set before us, looking to Jesus...' (verses 1, 2, RSV)

The words gave an opening for me to share for the first time how things had been over the past months. It was hard to put into words but the ladies listened with understanding and, far from criticism, I could feel their support and concern. Afterwards others felt able to share their difficulties of one kind or another and, by doing so, we were drawn even closer. It was a valuable morning and, for all my hesitancy, I would not have missed that openness together. Through shared adversity God had further strengthened our love for one another.

My birthday came round soon after this and I enjoyed going out to a garden centre restaurant with Les. The light lunch was delicious and the surroundings colourful, despite the wintry weather. Once home I began to open cards and gifts and, as I did so, was suddenly aware of that horrible 'injection feeling' which had plagued me so often in earlier months. I was upset that this should happen again, particularly on my birthday, and realized that it showed my ongoing vulnerability. In its wake I found myself getting over-anxious about trivia again, and troubled on various other fronts, most of all with the thought that I wasn't doing enough. Didn't the Bible exhort us: 'Never flag in zeal, be aglow with the Spirit, serve the Lord' (Romans 12:11, RSV)? What a useless life I seemed to be living in comparison with that, and with many of my friends. This greatly troubled me until I sat and wrote a list of all the things I was doing. Perhaps it wasn't such a useless life after all? As for the words from Romans – well, I realized that this was a general exhortation but that there are times when, for a while, God has a different agenda for us. A set-aside period perhaps? Could I accept this and stop berating myself?

At my next appointment the doctor cautioned me again about doing too much, but was pleased with my gradual progress, although the anti-depressant medication needed to be slightly stepped up. Also, I was put back on a drug to combat the nausea, which was again making me feel unwell and causing pain.

The setback on my birthday (which lasted for several days) had unnerved me, particularly because it had interrupted an encouraging trend. It was important to rest it with God and so find some relief for my apprehension. (Is this going to keep on happening?) I realized again that it was important to try and live closely with Jesus, one day at a time. My mind went back to the beautiful psalm picture of the small child nestled against its mother, trusting and at peace, living in the 'now'. I was also helped by these words:

'...For my part I know that I am in the hands of a wise and loving God...the fact implies a purpose interwoven in the fabric of life. God, none the less, does not expect me to twist my mind to discover a pattern, where, too close to the tapestry, I cannot yet trace it' (E.M. Blaiklock, *Kathleen*).

No, I couldn't trace any pattern in this long adversity, though I was aware of many God-given blessings – silver threads so carefully chosen and woven through the dark fabric of a hard experience.

*****

One morning in late January I decided to brave the snowy weather and take a trip to the city. Les was busy invigilating for exams at the Academy and I didn't want to be at home alone all day, tempted to think 'me' thoughts. I hadn't been back to town since that difficult shopping day in November, and now wanted to discover that, with the improvement, I could tackle such a challenge again. This time I took the bus to avoid the strain of driving, and planned a list that only stretched from 1–6. The trip went well. I made my way from shop to shop in leisurely fashion and then, to celebrate, treated myself to a bowl of soup and a slice of cheesecake. Once home I sat by the fireside for a while enjoying Jesus' presence, grateful for his help, and much reassured.

Next time I found those irrational fears and anxieties creeping back I pictured my tired, troubled mental processes as sloughing away, to be completely discarded as Jesus' gift of new healed thoughts replaced them. Rather like a butterfly's emergence from an old confining cocoon to delightful freedom and freshness. 'One day I will leave the old cocoon behind,' I told myself. 'Then it won't enclose and imprison me anymore.'

This thought helped as I moved on into the coming weeks. Soon the first snowdrops lifted their fragile heads to February's chill winds and, as I looked at them trembling in the front flowerbed, hope continued to grow. Yes, as my friend had said, those exquisite flowers had been forming beneath the cold earth all through the long winter, but now they were determined to herald better days. And the days were slowly getting better for me. What a relief!

One day I sat and considered the ways in which improvement was evident, at least for most of the time. I was more relaxed, less driven, and had come to accept that there were things I couldn't do just yet – but none the less many that I could. A measure of confidence had returned so that I had even begun to start this writing project, and had also led an informal group at which I had spoken about favourite hymns. Irrational fears were less frequent and more easily overcome. Decision-making wasn't nearly so difficult – I didn't usually dither in the supermarket now.

These developments slowly continued over the

spring weeks, though I was still aware of being vulnerable. A sudden change in programme tended to throw me and I became agitated on occasions, particularly when a meeting dragged on, or a shop queue hardly moved. My concentration remained poor and wandering thoughts were a particular nuisance at church, or when I was trying to take in a chunk of the Bible or a chapter of a devotional book. One of my prayer partners lent me cassette recordings of the New Testament in a dramatized form, with background music and these have proved most helpful; I am still happily working my way through the New Testament. My thoughts remained scattered at times, so that my mind flitted from one thing to the next without any logical connection. 'Some of these symptoms are partly due to the medication,' the doctor explained, so that was reassuring. My mind *will* get back to normal!

There continue to be occasional interruptions to this upward trend, days when the darkness threatens again. At one such recent time my two prayer partners visited and offered the opportunity to share the fears and frustrations that had again begun to press on my mind. Being able to tell them (it was hard to find words at times) brought immediate relief, as did their sensitive prayers. I could feel their love for me and, once again, this helped restore self-worth. Later I pondered how such prayer times enabled me to be hopeful, more constructive in my thinking. It's very important to develop a healthy attitude towards illness!

The next day Les and I took a drive across country, stopping en route to walk along the banks of a gurgling stream, and then up over a small wooded hill. I was so glad to be in better physical form. Our drive then took us toward the mountains, still covered with snow, and on through a small town beside the River Dee, where we stopped for a snack. Cheesecake again for me! I came home refreshed and grateful. Yes, whatever my circumstances, there was still so much to enjoy!

8. WHAT DIRECTION AHEAD?

There's a big question in my mind now as improvement continues. Will this depressive illness go for good, never to return? I long very much that it will and, since it has had a physical trigger, it would seem likely that the easing of this latter problem will result in permanent relief of the depression. At a recent hospital visit I discovered that the physical difficulty is chronic pancreatitis – a condition that cannot be cured but can be eased significantly with the drug treatment I am receiving. That reassured me.

Ultimately the answer regarding permanent healing – physical as well as mental – rests with God, and I have full confidence in him. He knows the deep yearning of my heart, he has heard the many requests. Surely all is well when trusted to him?

So the more important questions are – What will I take with me as I journey on? What have I gained of permanent value? As someone has put it:

'Let me read with open eyes the book my days are writing – and learn' (Dag Hammarskjold, *Markings*).

I can take empathy with me now, as distinct from sympathy. The hard learning has taught me, at least to some extent, the anguish of depressive illness. It has given me the desire to care, share and identify with others in similar straits and I want to do so with a willing and tender heart.

Then there has been the profound humbling. The recognition that I am as vulnerable as anyone else. This has been a hard acknowledgement, but the following words are reassuring: 'The final humiliation of the human spirit is in accepting the fact that God knows what we are like and loves us as we are' (Bishop Stephen Bayne).

Most of all the long, bewildering journey has drawn me closer to Jesus. I love him for all that he has been to me, all that he will yet be. I would not have wanted to miss this rich experience, even though the way to it has been exacting in the extreme. John Newton, after many difficulties, put it so well: 'If it were possible for me to alter any part of his plan, I could only spoil it.'

And so I journey on along the route that began more than a year ago when seemingly insignificant circumstances set me off in a completely new, untravelled direction. But I am not alone. Jesus has never left me, and he never will. All is well; and all will be well.

9. ARE YOU TRYING TO HELP A PERSON SUFFERING FROM A DEPRESSIVE ILLNESS?

Here are some hints which might be relevant:

DON'T ask 'How are you?' That is a difficult question to answer with honesty, and in a sentence or two. DO ask 'How have you felt today?' 'How has this week been?' That is much easier to cope with.

STEER CLEAR of 'I never thought *you'd* fall for that,' whether spoken or implied. It triggers needless guilt and distress.

NEVER SAY – 'Snap out of it!' You wouldn't use those words to someone with appendicitis etc. This sufferer is ill too.

NEVER SAY – 'Surely it can't be as bad as that?' How do you know? Mental anguish is intensely painful.

STEER CLEAR OF – 'What reason have you got to be depressed when other people are suffering so much more?' This comment not only implies a complete lack of sympathy but it also induces needless, unhelpful guilt.

DO assure of your prayers, specially when a doctor's appointment or a new challenge has to be faced. Be careful to follow-through on the promise.

DO be available if asked 'Will you come and pray with me?' or 'May I visit you?'

DO send an affectionate note, and maybe a quotation or a brief hymn. Go cautiously with Bible verses. One friend confided, 'I'm tired of kindly-meant Bible quotes, they frustrate me in my present state of mind.'

DO give flowers or other small gifts, just as you would to any other ill person. You may be stuck for words but such gifts speak most appropriately instead.

DO call in with some home-baking or a pot of soup. These tempt a poor appetite and convey your care in an unforgettable way.

DO offer light reading, magazines, puzzle books. Music cassettes or recorded books (and the New Testament) can also be a big help. Don't swamp the person, however! Then, as well, it has meant much when a friend has stopped to read me a short section from a book or from the Bible.

DON'T offer your favourite theological tomes, even if they do give a helpful angle on suffering etc. Any heavy books are inadvisable, and also those that have an accusatory/corrective tone. I struggled through one of these and it left me even more depressed.

DO offer an impromptu outing. A country drive with a coffee stop perhaps?

DO show affection. A touch of the hand, a warm hug, a kiss conveys so much more than words. It assures a person that they're loved, valued and accepted, even though circumstances have bowled them right over.

DO offer humour as/when appropriate. A funny story or a humourous book lightens the day and laughter is very therapeutic. (I needed to be open to it, however.)

DO offer a listening, sympathetic ear, even if it means sitting silent for a long time. (Never look at your watch!) This offered gift of time and the opportunity to release pent up fears and feelings is much appreciated, and the outcome very beneficial. This is one of the greatest ways in which you can help.

While listening DON'T give any shocked glances or look askance at the sufferer.

After listening DON'T offer advice, unless asked, and never dismiss or belittle fears. Instead a perceptive comment may well be helpful and will reveal understanding.

DON'T watch and wait for evidence of a scattered, forgetful mind. It is hard to feel as if you are under surveillance. Never comment on failings or inefficiencies, to the person concerned or to others. Instead come alongside with love and helpfulness.

DO show genuine understanding when a person can't fulfil a commitment, even though they *seem* well enough. Continually make allowances, and offer reassurance.

DO encourage the person to take up an activity or helping task that is within their range, and share pleasure at their progress, even if it is slow and intermittent.

Above all, keep on BELIEVING IN THEM AND FOR THEM. Stay with them all the way, through eager progress and lengthy setbacks. DON'T get tired of caring for them, nor allow concern to diminish. A person with a depressive illness needs to know that you are still rooting for them, whatever.